THE RUNNIEST BOOK YOU'LL EVER FEED!

For example. . . .

Did you hear the one about the teaching assistant who offered to help her new students in the introductory calculus course with their graphing problems?

"Work out the problem on your own," she advised, "then come to me and I'll graph it for you."

Student Jack was a bit put off when he went to her with his solution and was told he'd have to wait, because there were other students ahead of him.

"I'm sorry," the teacher admonished him, "but my policy on this is strictly first sum, first curved."

BUT WAIT!

THERE'S MORE!

READ ON. *(Take my book, please!)*

PARDON ME ROY, AND OTHER GROANERS

by
Robert C. Cumbow

Illustrations
by
Arthur Howard

PINNACLE BOOKS NEW YORK

Although the main characters in this book were real people, and the events herein depicted did take place, in some instances both the people and the events were fictionally intensified to add to the drama of the story.

PARDON ME ROY AND OTHER GROANERS

Copyright © 1983 by Robert C. Cumbow

An original Pinnacle Books edition, published for the first time anywhere.

First printing, July, 1983

ISBN: 0-523-42040-4

Cover illustration by Scott Ross

Printed in the United States of America

PINNACLE BOOKS, INC.
1430 Broadway
New York, New York 10018

This Collection Is Dedicated
to
The Collectors
—Somebody finally wrote them all down!

RCC

PARDON ME ROY, AND OTHER GROANERS

PARDON ME ROY, AND OTHER GROANERS

An Introduction

Joke fads come and go.

In my life, I remember many with nostalgic fondness. Little Moron Jokes ("Why did the Little Moron put his father in the freezer?" "He wanted to have an ice-cold pop!"). Bloody Marys ("Mommy, what's a werewolf?" "Shut up and comb your face!"). Doll jokes ("The Liz Taylor Doll: Wind it up and it files for divorce"). Tom Swifties ("They've cut off diplomatic relations with us," said Tom, disconsolately). Marriages ("If Barbra Streisand married David Seville, she'd be Barbra Seville!"). Elephant Jokes ("What's red and white on the outside and gray on the inside?" "A can of Campbell's Cream of Elephant Soup") and their offbeat progeny, the Fruit-and-Vegetable Jokes ("What's round and purple and hums?" "An electric grape." "What's long and orange and goes click-click, click-click?" "A ball-point carrot."). And that funny but cruel development of the Little Moron Joke known as the Polack Joke, which died almost overnight when suddenly the Pope was Polish and Solidarity was an issue of world interest.

This kind of joke craze, like a fly, is born, grows old, and dies in a relatively short period of time. But there's another genre of joke that's never been in the forefront of contemporary humor, but has enjoyed a devoted and growing following in the joke-telling underground for years. The best way I can illustrate the genre is by retelling the first one I ever heard:

There was an old Indian chief, so the story goes, who took particular delight in fat things. All three of his wives were quite stout; he rode a fat horse, and ate a lot of pork. In his declining years, the members of his tribe gave him, as a special gift, a trip to Africa. There, he made the acquaintance of the chief of a native people. Upon learning of the Indian chief's fetish, the African tribesman presented his new friend with a special tribute: a hippopotamus skin. Proudly, the chief brought it home with him to America and placed it on the floor of his lodge especially for the comfort of his Number One Wife. At 300 pounds, she was the biggest woman in the tribe. A little further back from her and the chief sat wives number two and three, one on a buffalo skin, the other on an elk skin. They held positions of less honor in the chief's world, because they were not quite so fat, weighing only 250 and 225 respectively. Nevertheless, they were still portly enough to please the chief, and he took great pride in them. "I *am*, however, worried about my sons," he confided to his shaman. "They seem puny. They weigh only 150 pounds each. That is probably because they are the sons of my second and third wives. Had I only had a child by my Number One Wife, *there* would have been a son! Why, these two boys weigh only half what she does!" The medicine man, whose thoughts seemed elsewhere, suddenly brightened. He rose and shouted, "That proves it!" The chief was puzzled. "Proves what?" he asked. "What I've always suspected," said the shaman triumphantly: "The squaw on the hippopotamus is equal to the sons of the squaws on the other two hides!"

I first encountered that story in the late '50s. I think it was in a Bennett Cerf

collection, but I'm not sure. At the time it was little more than a clever, elaborately prepared pun. I didn't think of it then as the grandfather of an entire subgenre.

But on one slow spring day Mr. Thomas J. Sanderson told an eighth grade boys' music class at Heidelberg American Junior High School another story that fit the same pattern (that story, which I call "A Disaster of State," can be found in the anthology that follows). I began to see the possibilities.

As the years passed, what had seemed to be a couple of quirky forced puns grew into a whole species of funny story. Once in a while I'd run across a full-fledged *collector*. Dianne Bye at Seattle University in 1967. Alan Ehmann at the Upstairs Theatre Downtown in El Paso in 1970. Art Chamberlin—pilot, naval officer, writer —in Seattle in 1972. J.E. "Al" Lasater of the Washington State Department of Fisheries, during the mid-'70s. Mike Caffarel, communications executive, then of Seattle, now of New Jersey, in 1979. Doug McFarland, who puts them on the marquee of Seattle's Phillips Scale Co.

Wherever people like these would congregate for a joke session, these puns would be swapped until each participant had told all he could remember. Everyone would go home with new specimens stored safely away; and someone would always say,

"Someday somebody ought to write all these down somewhere." Every once in a while one *would* appear in print—as a filler in somebody's newsletter, perhaps, or a "laugh of the day." Wordmaster Edwin Newman confessed to a weakness for puns in one of his books, and was pleased by a couple I sent him in the mail. Every so often Emmett Watson would print one in his Seattle Post *Intelligencer* column.

Then in 1980, two of the old chestnuts of the genre turned up in Willard Espy's *Another Almanac of Words at Play*, the contribution of puzzler-jokester Arnold Moss. And though neither of the jokes was new to me, Espy's volume was the first to give these jokes a name, as far as I knew. The redoubtable Willard called them "Puns in Perpetuity," defining them simply as "puns that require elaborate buildups." I guess that's the fairest and briefest definition that could be given. For a while, I called them "hippopotamuses," after the Squaw story. The term seemed appropriate to the narrative bloat that attends the telling of this kind of tale.

The buildup may be long, but should not be long-*winded*. Even if comparatively short, it should be far-fetched; yet the art of telling (and creating) these stories is to make the set-up seem reasonable, and— through use of synonyms and circumlocution—to avoid giving away the punchline betimes. A friend of mine calls them "baroque puns" because the telling is nothing if not a systematic process of ornamenting—and thereby justifying—what is essentially an outrageous one-liner.

Why this kind of joke is both funny and *more than funny* is not for me to say. I will acknowledge that its success is measured as much in groans as in smiles; but I caution you that even the most outrageous of these creations must be *legitimate*. The listener can't feel he's been cheated, or led afield to no purpose. The joke comes off best if he gets a sense of having tripped *himself* up somewhere along the way. The details with which the story is embellished must not be there purely to distract, but must be reasonably related to story and punchline.

The punchline itself is not usually a simple pun but a Spoonerized or otherwise mangled rendition of some familiar phrase— usually a famous cliche, proverb, or quotation. The finish is presented as "the moral of the story" in the classic form, which is why Mary Ann Madden was moved to call the genre "Fractured Fables" in a *New York* Magazine competition a few years ago (results of that competition, and of many others, appear in her book *Maybe He's Dead*, Random House, 1981, and will be of interest to fellow collectors as well as dabblers in the form). Professor William T. Rabe of Punsters Unlimited (c/o The Unicorn Hunters Conglomerate, Lake Superior State College, Sault Ste. Marie, Michigan 49783, in case you're interested in his wonderful pun-protecting and preserving operation) confers the name "Groaner" on this form. That suits me just fine.

Got some of your own devising, dear reader? Please send them along, in care of the publisher.

ROBERT C. CUMBOW
c/o Pinnacle Books
1430 Broadway
New York NY 10018

The groaners in this collection represent jokes that I've heard in many different versions. In each case, I've chosen the version that seems to me best in the telling; but there's been no effort to be definitive here, just to have—and spread—a little fun. If you find weeds among these flowers, be kind: Cast them aside, the better to reap the full benefit of the sweeter blooms. That's right: Weed 'em and reap.

HAPPY TRAILS TO YOU

On their anniversary, Dale Evans bought Roy Rogers a beautiful gift: A pair of superbly hand-tooled boots of the finest leather. Needless to say, Roy was more than pleased, and put them on for a ride around the spread. Somewhere out on the south forty, as Trigger carried him at a walk between a couple large outcroppings of rock, there was suddenly a loud scream. From one of the rocks leapt a sizable mountain lion, and caught Roy by the foot before he had time to react. The weight of the cat knocked Roy off Trigger onto the ground; and as Roy tried to kick the mountain lion away, the beast kept snapping violently about his ankles and feet. Trigger, startled, reared up and managed to frighten the mountain lion back into the rocks. Roy struggled to his feet, got back on Trigger, and made his way back to the house. He was all right, except for a few lacerations; but the brand new boots were, of course, ruined. Dale bandaged Roy's ankles, but she couldn't console him over the loss of the boots. While they sat together, she trying to comfort him, there came a knock at the door. In came the ranch foreman, dragging behind him the body of a large mountain lion he'd just killed. Said he: "Pardon me, Roy—is this the cat that chewed your new shoes?"

Thanks to Mark Goldfarb

A DISASTER OF STATE

The faroff kingdom of Oomgaway held the distinction of being a democratic monarchy. Its king, the benevolent Bungadayo, was ruler not by birth but by a free vote of the people. Each year the entire population of Oomgaway—not a large place, by any means—would emerge from their grass huts to caucus and elect a new king. But so happy were they with the wisdom and gentleness of Bungadayo's rule that they re-elected him every time.

Nevertheless, they stuck to a time-honored tradition: Each year, following the election, they would present the king with a brand new throne, made of bamboo, balsa, or some other light, dried wood, thatched together with grass. Bungadayo would rule proudly from his ceremonial throne all year; and when election time rolled around, and he was presented with a new throne, he'd store the old one away. He couldn't bear to discard these old thrones, since they held great sentimental value; and besides, to get rid of them would be a great insult to the workmen who had built them.

As the thrones piled up, Bungadayo finally found it advantageous to have a special warehouse constructed for the purpose of stashing away the used thrones. This was not difficult, as all houses in Oomgaway were made of woven, thatched grass. For years the procedure remained the same: Bungadayo would be re-elected, he'd receive a new throne, and the old one would be deposited in the warehouse with the others. The thrones grew great in number, as did the years of Bungadayo's enlightened rule.

One day, however, as misfortune would have it, one of the king's attendants went into the warehouse at night, looking for something, and he lighted his way with a torch. With the brittle, dry wood of Bungadayo's many accumulated thrones inside, the warehouse almost instantly burst into flame. The explosion was so great that it set the palace and many nearby homes ablaze; these in turned fired others; and it was only a short time before the entire capital city of Oomgaway—which was, in fact, the whole of Oomgaway itself—was burned to the ground. Only a handful of people survived, and the great kingdom of Oomgaway was never re-established.

The moral of the story: People who live in grass houses shouldn't stow thrones.

Thanks to Tom Sanderson

AUTHOR AND PUBLISHER

The publisher was dismayed at the manuscript for Robert Louis Stevenson's *A Child's Garden of Verses*. He'd contracted for a children's book, of course, but he was appalled that Stevenson had delivered a volume of *poetry*. "It'll never sell," said the publisher, and informed Stevenson that he was backing out of the contract. Stevenson, however, gently reminded him he had no leg to stand on: "After all," said the author, "I never promised you a prose garden."

THE STRAWBERRY AS BIG AS THE RITZ

A farmer was dismayed to discover, one morning, an enormous strawberry growing in one of his strawberry patches. Not just your usual, ordinary enormous strawberry, but a gargantuan, record-shattering, Believe-It-Or-Not granddaddy of all enormous strawberries: It must have been four feet in diameter!

The farmer got on the phone right away to report this oddity to the Department of Agriculture, and was told that an agent would be out right away to inspect the strawberry and give the farmer his assessment. After a short time, a government car pulled up in the drive, and the farmer went out to greet a pleasant-looking young man and escort him to the strawberry patch.

The young man's eyes indeed boggled at the sight of the strawberry. He'd seen outsized fruit before, but this was incredible. "Think that thing's worth some money?" asked the farmer, pleased with himself. "Probably plenty," agreed the agent. "Any idea how much?" the farmer asked. The agent replied, "It'll take me a while to work that out. I didn't expect anything quite so big." He started hauling measuring tapes, tools, calipers, clipboards, charts and books out of his car.

The farmer watched awhile, as the young man measured this way and that, took readings, recorded, calculated. Finally the agent said, "Look, this is still going to take a little longer. It's pretty dull stuff, but it has to be done. Why don't you go on back inside and relax? I'll let you know when I'm finished, and tell you what I've figured out." The farmer agreed, and shuffled back up to his house, where he settled into his favorite chair to wait. He couldn't see the strawberry patch from the window, but he *could* see the edge of the driveway, and the agriculture man's car sitting there; and after what seemed like a very long time, he was startled to see the young man stumbling up the drive toward his car *carrying the huge strawberry on his back*!

In a flash the farmer was out of his chair and out the door, shouting, "Wait! What do you think you're doin' there, mister?" Caught in the act, the agent turned and shot the farmer a withering sneer. "Can't you guess?" he asked. "I came to *seize* your berry, not appraise it."

THE NUN'S STORY

Back in the early '60s, when Soeur Sourire, "The Singing Nun," was popular, she was quite a hot item on the concert circuit for awhile. One day she happened to show up at the office of a booking agent to sign on for a Borscht Belt tour. Coming in at the same time, for the same purpose, was comedian Shelley Berman. An aggressive and impatient sort, Berman hurried forward to put pen to paper and get on with his business. In so doing, he rudely edged the sister aside; but the agent would have none of this behavior in his office. "Hold on," he said firmly. "Wait 'til the nun signs, Shelley."

DON'T MESS WITH
THE HARDWARE

A Science Fiction Story

On a distant asteroid, in a galaxy far, far away, lives a computer-ruled society, whose virtual Utopia is based on the fact that whatever anyone wants or needs, whatever problem requires solving, satisfaction is only as far away as the nearest computer terminal. These terminals are known as "Ask-Its," for obvious reasons. If a person needs to ask the computer a question, he simply proceeds to his nearest Ask-It and "asks it."

But there is always the danger of misuse or overuse by citizens, so the terminals are designed occasionally to shut down for cooling and self-repair. One day a hermit, who had lived for years in the hills, far from the nearest Ask-It, came into town with a number of questions and problems he'd been accumulating for some time. Hoping to get all his needs taken care of in one session, he approached the nearest terminal and began to input question after question. Things went smoothly for a while; but when he was almost finished with his job a warning light came on, signalling the danger of an overload. Nevertheless, the hermit persisted in putting questions and requests into the Ask-It.

Soon a message appeared on the screen instructing the hermit to discontinue his input, and take the remainder of his job to a different terminal. But the hermit ignored this also, and continued to push buttons and shout information into the terminal. At last, the terminal employed its most extreme self-protection mechanism: A laser beam shot from the Ask-It and reduced the hermit to cinders, canceling the entire transaction.

The moral of the story: Don't put all your begs in one Ask-It.

A PRIVATE AQUARIUM

Dabney had an unusual hobby: He collected and studied porpoises. He was wealthy enough to maintain a large saltwater pool in his basement, and as the years went by the porpoises in it seemed to grow younger rather than older. A friend of Dabney's, a marine biologist, examined the animals and was astonished. "The state of these porpoises is incredible," he told the rich man. "If they're really as old as you say, their health and condition don't show it at all. I don't know what your secret is, but it seems as if, as long as the porpoises stay here in this pool, well fed and happy, they'll live forever."

Dabney didn't know what the secret was either, but he was delighted to learn that his porpoises were immortal, and decided to concentrate on expanding his marine collection to other forms of life as well. He added some fish, a few crabs, some seaweed. Then he hit upon the perfect finishing touch: A smattering of seagulls added to the basement "ocean" would give him a perfect marine environment!

He drove to the coast and acquired a dozen seagulls. But upon arriving home, he found the neighborhood in quite a stir. A lion had escaped from the nearby zoo, and was sitting on his porch. It had done no damage, but it refused to be moved, and threatened everyone who came near. As Dabney puzzled what to do, a truck arrived from the zoo, and out jumped a team of guards, armed with pistols. These were the kind of guns that fire darts dipped in a sedative, and in a short time the guards had shot a dose into the lion, who summarily collapsed across the porch in a stupor.

Relieved, and eager to get his new seagulls into his basement as quickly as possible, Dabney dashed forward and stepped across the body of the dazed lion toward his front door. Before he could open it, however, he was frozen in his tracks by a firm voice: "Hold it, mister. You're under arrest." As the cuffs were snapped onto his wrists, Dabney demanded to know the charge. "Isn't it obvious?" asked the officer. "Transporting gulls across a staid lion for immortal porpoises."

Thanks to Dianne Bye

THE INEBRIATE

Two grasshoppers from the country were in town on a holiday, going from bar to bar, having a good time, but managing to hold their liquor pretty well. Much better, certainly, than a friend of theirs, a chigger, who was deep in his cups when they came across him on the street, between bars. He came forward, smiling, to greet them, but staggered, passed out, and rolled into the gutter. The chigger's wife came running up and began trying to rouse him. "I can't understand it," she told the grasshoppers. He had only one drink, and suddenly he was giggling, then crying, then trying to tear the bar down with his hands, and finally he ran into the street and just passed out like this." One grasshopper was amazed. "All that on just one drink?" he asked. The other was blasé: "You know what they say," he replied: "Chiggers can't be boozers."

TABOO

The safari party had become hopelessly lost, and by the third day had to stop to replenish their provisions in some way. "There appears to be an animal's lair up there," said one of the hunters. "Perhaps we can find food." The head bearer grew afraid at this. "No," he warned. "That is the cave of the dreaded Foo. Taboo. A horrible fate awaits those who go there."

But everything around them was a tangle of seemingly impenetrable foliage, and the hunters decided among themselves to pursue the course of least resistance, defy the taboo, and try to find food in the home of the Foo. The bearers ran off in terror, leaving the hunters to take the risky measure on their own. As they approached the cave, there came a great screeching and squawking, and out flew an enormous bird, with a wingspan on which all of the hunters could have sat comfortably.

Nevertheless, they were undaunted. One of the hunters said, "So this is the great Foo—nothing but an overgrown bird. I can handle that. And just think! One of its eggs could feed us for weeks!" But as they approached the cave, the Foo circled, swooped low, and loosened its bowels, dropping a great heap of guano that completely covered the hunting party.

By the time they groped their way out of the mess, the Foo was gone. Each of the hunters was covered with a coat of the great bird's leavings. They tried to clean themselves off with branches and leaves, but these proved inadequate to the task. Then they tried to sandpaper the stuff off with rocks, but it wouldn't be removed. They found a stream and bathed thoroughly in it, but emerged still coated with the Foo's droppings.

By this time the bearers had returned, bringing with them their tribal shaman, as a safeguard against the broken taboo. The bearers dared not draw close to the soiled hunters, however—partly because they had violated the taboo, and partly because they smelled awful. "We've tried everything!" wailed one of the hunters. "How do we get this stuff off of us?" "Won't *come* off," grunted the shaman. "Won't come *off*?" asked another hunter, incredulously. "What are we supposed to do?" "That's the taboo," said the shaman: "If the Foo shits, wear it."

A DOMESTIC QUARREL

A man and a woman looked dolefully out their apartment window, bemoaning the fact that a turn in the weather had spoiled their plans. "We could be out picnicking if it weren't for this hail," said she. "It's true our day's been ruined," replied he, "but this is *rain*, not hail." The wife looked quizzically at the husband, then out the window again. "You're surely mistaken, dear," she said, "This is definitely hail." "Nonsense!" said the husband, growing testy. "It's *rain*, my dear, pure and simple." "It's hail, my dear." "Darling, it's rain!" They bickered a moment; then the husband said, "Will you accept the judgment of a third party, dear?" When his wife agreed, he said, "Very well—we'll ask Rudolf."

Rudolf, a Russian immigrant, lived in the apartment upstairs. He was a great believer in the Soviet revolution, but had fled the country when an opposing faction had come to power. Amid the trappings of the revolutionist memorabilia with which he decorated his room, Rudolf listened as the husband and wife told their two views of the nature of the precipitation. Then he strolled to the window, took a look, and decreed, "I see no hail." The husband rose and shouted triumphantly at his wife, "You see? Rudolf the Red knows rain, dear!"

THE ILL-FATED REPLICA

A prize-winning scientist, praised for his work in genetic engineering, saved his greatest work for himself: He made a clone of himself, which enabled him to carry on his research and still keep all his appointments and lecture engagements. His clone, however, developed a weakness for liquor that the professor didn't have; and, upon becoming drunk, would begin to talk dirty and tell offensive stories. He took special delight in doing this when there were ladies present, and the whole thing became quite a scandal.

The professor finally managed to figure out why he was losing so many friends and so much of the respect that had once been his. He decided he'd have to get rid of his replica, before it caused him permanent embarrassment. He sent it off to a party one night, and then followed it by a couple of hours, arriving just when the creature was at its foulest. Seizing the replica by its ear, the professor hurled it down a flight of stairs; whereupon he was promptly placed under arrest by a police officer at the scene. The charge? Making an obscene clone fall.

ON-THE-JOB INJURY

Two stonemasons were puzzling over what to do about a huge chunk of rock that neither of them could lift. "I think we ought to get Nate's help," said one. "He can lift anything. He'll be able to help us move it." The other one didn't like that idea. "We don't need to get him to do our work for us," he said. "We can accomplish this scientifically, using the principle of the lever."

As his companion watched, he constructed a fulcrum and lever, and worked the end of the lever under the piece of rock. "Now, you'll see," he said; but when he pried down on the lever to lift the rock, he found it still wouldn't budge, and, trying to force it, he suffered a severe hernia that put him in the hospital for a week.

His friend, left behind with the rock still to be moved, fell back on his first plan and called for help from his buddy Nate, a big man who came over and easily helped the mason lift the stone.

The moral of the story: Better Nate than lever.

A ZOO STORY

"You aren't going to believe your eyes," said the zookeeper to the visiting research scientist as they hurried along the path toward the gnu's compound. "This animal actually *makes* these things, all by itself?" asked the scientist. "You'll see," said the keeper.

They arrived at the gnu enclosure. Inside stood a large, sleepy-eyed gnu, lazily chewing a mouthful of grass. The scientist looked the beast over very carefully. "He appears normal in every way," said the zookeeper, "but just watch this." The keeper opened the gate and tossed in several chunks of colored tile, a chunk of wood, and a tube of glue. The gnu eyed the stuff a moment or two, then sidled over and sat down. He began selecting different sizes and shapes and colors of tile, mixing and matching, and gluing them onto the chunk of wood. In a short time, before the disbelieving eyes of the scientist, the gnu had constructed a beautiful mosaic pattern.

"That's the most amazing thing I've ever seen," said the scientist. "Yes, and he's been doing it for months," said the zookeeper. "Over in the office we have hundreds of samples of his work." "Either he's been carefully trained," said the scientist, "or he's an extremely exceptional animal." "No," the zookeeper said: "He's a typical gnu and a tiler, too."

Thanks to Mike Caffarel

REMEMBERING HIS OWN

A young Indian left his reservation to go to school in the city. He took up electrical engineering, and after several years of study became one of the foremost students in his field. Nevertheless, before he accepted any of the big job offers that came his way, he insisted on returning home to the reservation to do one important job.

"It's always bothered me," he said, "that there's no electricity in the toilet in the tribal center. You can't see when you use it at night. I'm going to fix that." And he proceeded to install a complete system of electrical wiring and outlets for the lavatory. When the job was done, he went his way, took a big job, and became one of the most famous names in electrical engineering.

"But why did he take the time to do that little job?" people asked. "Any do-it-yourself electrician could have done it. Why did he take time out from his career to do that?" Well, it's because he had heard that the first thing you should always do is to wire a head for a reservation.

THE SIGN OF RANK

Another Science Fiction Story

The astronauts of the Saturn-probe were astonished to find that the mysterious planet was populated by millions of tiny, fuzzy creatures who could actually communicate with them in English. "We are called the Furries," said the Saturnian spokesman, and the captain of the Saturn-probe had to admit it was an appropriate name. The little creatures were irresistably cute, tiny balls of fluff with big eyes blinking out from their middles and tiny feet sticking out at the bottom. "Well," said the captain to the Furry who had addressed him, "take us to your leader." "Easily done," said the Furry, pointing out a large Furry whose head was improbably adorned with a large hypodermic needle sticking into the air. "He's the Furry with the syringe on top."

THE WITCH'S CURSE

Benny, a sailor traveling in a distant and exotic land, ran afoul of a wicked witch he met there, and she placed a curse on him. "Never again shall you dare to cut your beard," she declaimed, "or a terrible fate will befall you." The curse seemed preposterous; and Benny believed neither in witches nor in curses. Still, just to be on the safe side, he left his beard untrimmed. It was his natural style anyway, and he saw no reason to change. It was a luxury not having to shave; and as the years went by Benny's beard grew to a size that earned him international renown.

One day, however, he met a lovely and respectable young lady, with whom he fell deeply in love. She had eyes for him as well, but their burgeoning relationship was impaired by her aversion to his famous beard. At last she delivered the ultimatum: It had to be her or the beard. She won, and Benny proceeded to the shaving bowl, razor in hand. He was gone a long time—*too* long, in fact. His friends began to worry, and when their knocks went unanswered, they broke into the bathroom. Instead of Benny, they found only a huge funeral urn, its tiled sides looking for all the world like a permanently frozen visage of the hapless sailor.

The moral of the story: A Benny shaved is a Benny urned.

RESEARCH

A candidate for a doctoral degree in pharmacological psychology was doing intensive research on the effects of marijuana. His unique approach was to test the substance on a variety of animals. In one phase of his project, he was feeding large quantities of marijuana to sea birds. For weeks he'd been wandering up and down the beaches and waterfronts, capturing the birds and administering the drug. Before releasing the birds, he'd tag them with a band around the neck, so he could tell which ones had partaken. Whenever he saw one of those sea birds without a tag, he'd spare no effort to capture it and give it a dose. It was his intention to leave no tern unstoned.

PERFORMANCE CANCELED

The high point of the Latini Brothers' magic act was the point when Mario and Giulio caused brother Sergio to float in midair. All three brothers did other things, of course—small feats of prestidigitation and minor illusions—but that act of levitation was the big draw. Night after night the customers came to see it. Sergio, alas, had a weakness for the grape, and one night showtime found him in his cups. He was so hopelessly drunk, he couldn't go on; and without him, the act would have no finale. Sadly, Mario had to go onstage and tell the audience: "He who levitates is sauced."

HAVING A BOLL

A distinguished boll weevil in a large cotton field had an eligible daughter, whom he wished to marry well. He picked out a fine young weevil to court her—one of only two eligible bachelors in the entire field. He was an accomplished young weevil, with many bolls to his credit, and everyone agreed he was a comer. The other bachelor, by contrast, was a layabout, with no ambition, no source of income. He was content to live on the remnants of the other weevils' industriousness.

Unfortunately for her father, the daughter became enamored of the layabout weevil, and while she was carrying on her flirtation with him, the industrious young weevil went off and married someone else. When mating season arrived, only the layabout was left for the daughter to marry, and what had been a harmless flirtation became her way of life. Her father was bitterly disappointed, but he was firm with her: "It's a shame," he said, "but you had to settle for the lesser of two weevils."

SAVED BY THE R.A.F.

Alfie and Freddie were making the rounds of the alehouses, determined to have a pint in each and every pub in their part of town, or be carried home unconscious for trying. They'd just left the *Pig and Duck* and were on their way to the *Bird and Bush* when they found their way blocked by nothing less than a large African lion. "Now 'ow 're we goin' t' get t' the *Bird 'n Bush*," moaned Freddie, "wi' *that* in the way?" Alfie was in favor of making a detour: "Let's cut across to the *Toad in th' 'Ole*. Maybe by the time we've 'ad a pint there, 'e'll be gone."

Freddie would have none of it. "I plotted our course carefully, to make sure we'd get the greatest number o' pints wi' the smallest amount o' walkin'," he said. "The Toad's several blocks outter our way, an' goin' there'll ruin me 'ole plan." As they stood there debating, the sky was suddenly filled with the sound of jet aircraft. Three of them dipped low out of formation, rolled between the rows of buildings, and opened up on the lion with machine guns. The lion roared out, then collapsed, dead. Alfie and Freddie waved their thanks to the planes, and continued uninterrupted to the *Bird and Bush*.

The moral of the story: The shortest distance between two pints is a strafed lion.

Thanks to Al Lasater

A CASE OF BURGLARY

The private detective listened with interest as his client, old Mr. Chan, told his incredible story. "A little boy has been coming into my house at night and stealing priceless pieces from my teak collection," he said. "How do you know it's a little boy?" asked the detective. "Easy," replied Chan. "Little footprints on the floor. He must come through the garden, getting his feet muddy."

A wealthy retired exporter, Chan had one of the world's most expensive collections of teakwood carvings, and was in a frenzy at seeing his collection diminished night after night, a piece at a time. Try as he might, though, he couldn't even catch sight of the thief, much less catch him.

The detective went to work, and after a few nights' vigil, was able to catch sight of the thief. He watched in amazement as a shadowy shape crept through the garden, into Chan's house, and across the room to the display shelves. As it reached a dark hand out for a new treasure, the detective switched on the lights. To his amazement, there stood no little boy but a small brown bear! The bear froze a moment, then recovered its composure, grabbed one of the teaks, and ran. As it did so, the detective saw to his amazement that it had no normal claws and pads, but a tiny pair of white, human feet protruding from its ankles!

It was a strange, disorienting sight, and one that (in a disturbing transposition of appendages) gave the detective pause. But in a moment he was up and after the culprit. He cornered the bear in Chan's yard, and drew his gun. Advancing upon the thief, he exulted, "I've got you now, boy-foot bear with teak of Chan!"

Thanks to Al Lasater

GENERATION GAP

Eschewing the customary British enthusiasm for cricket, one Londoner developed a mad passion for American baseball instead. So consuming was his interest that he moved his family to the United States and went to umpire school, in order to be as close as possible to the game he loved. But from the day he began umpiring games, his relationship with his little son deteriorated. Try as he might, he couldn't even get the boy to sit on his lap any longer. The kid abjectly refused. It seemed unreasonable; but the truth is that the son never sits on the British umpire.

UP THE CLOCK

In his later years, natural food specialist Euell Gibbons took to drinking, it's said, and developed a special affection for the popular Caribbean whipped rum and citrus concoction, which he would order up regularly in his local bar. Nevertheless, he never lost his taste for those wild hickory nuts, and so commissioned his bartender to come up with a way to blend the two tastes. The mixologist—a retired college professor whom everyone knew affectionately as "Doc"—ground up a fistful of the hickory nuts, and whipped them into the drink. The result was an instant success; and to this day in that particular bar, one can hear the order, "I'll have a hickory daiquiri, Doc!"

THE HOME REMEDY

"How can I show my horse at the county fair with a bird's nest in his mane?" asked the exasperated farmer. Lum took a long look, and sure enough, there was a nest of chirping birds ensconced in the horse's mane. "I've tried everything," said the farmer. "Washing, combing, fumigating, rubbing the hair down with the nastiest stuff I can think of. But no matter what I do, the bird's nest is back again the next day. How can I keep them out?"

"I'll tell you what you do," said Lum, after a long think. "You buy yourself a bunch of yeast, good old dry yeast, and rub it into that horse's mane just as thorough as you can, and see if that don't do the trick."

The farmer was pretty puzzled; but he'd tried everything else, so he decided to give Lum's suggestion a chance. That night he gave his horse's mane a thorough brush-down with the yeast, massaging it deep into the hair. Next day, when he checked the horse, the nest was gone! The birds had not returned. They didn't come back that day, or the next, or ever again.

The farmer was so impressed that he went back to Lum's store to say a personal thank-you. "But I'm dying to know," he added, "How does it work?" "Easy," said Lum. "Y'see, yeast is yeast, and nest is nest, and never the mane shall tweet."

Thanks to Dianne Bye

The mid-east land of Shoon is traditionally ruled by the Shinn. The Shinn of Shoon and his wife the Sheen lived in the ancestral palace, and their life was a good one, except for one thing. Their son, the heir, the Shan of Shoon, was ill. Often the lad would be taken with terrible seizures, and the Shinn lived in mortal terror that during one of these fits the boy would seriously injure himself. He therefore insisted that the Shan be guarded constantly.

One night, nevertheless, the dreaded thing happened. The little Shan had a terrible seizure and fell out of bed, striking his head on the marble floor of the nursery. As the boy lay in the hospital with a serious concussion, the Shinn called to him the captain of the guard, and demanded to know who was supposed to be guarding the Shan that night. Told it was Sergeant Fazool, whose weakness for drink was well known, the Shinn flew into a rage and called for the man to be brought before him.

The hapless Fazool was dragged into the Shinn's receiving room in a sorry state of disarray. With robes and scimitar flashing, the Shinn confronted the cowering Fazool. "Before I strike off your head," he said, "I have one question: Where were you when the fit hit the Shan?"

MISSING PERSON

A certain young lady met, at a party one night, a soft-spoken, good-hearted young Korean named Rhee. He was, he told her, a photographer for *Life* magazine, which only fascinated her all the more. She had a wonderful time with Rhee that night; and by the end of an enjoyable evening found herself quite taken with the man. The next day, she called the magazine to get hold of him again, but was told he'd been sent overseas on a dangerous assignment, and would be back in a few days. When he hadn't returned in a week, she called again and was informed that he'd been reported missing, and that a search had been mounted. So obsessed was she with Rhee by now that the lady insisted on joining the search herself. Good thing, too, for it was she who finally located Rhee, in an uncharted jungle hamlet where he lay recuperating from an injury. Overcome with emotion, she embraced him, crying, "Ah! Sweet Mr. Rhee of *Life*, at last I've found you!"

*Thanks to Arnold Moss, who told
a different version to Willard Espy*

TOUGH GIRL

A lusty country girl had a lot in the looks department, but was generally avoided by the local boys, because of her reputation for strong-arming men. It seems that, with a succession of suitors, she had expressed herself in an unorthodox manner if she didn't get her way: She'd punched them out, and so vigorously as to render them unconscious. Her reputation preceded her throughout the country: "She conks to stupor."

BASES ON BALLS

All-star pitcher Mel Famey was one of the best in baseball; but as he continued season after season to break his own records and maintain the high standards fans and teammates had come to expect, the pressure on him grew greater. During one particularly tense playoff game, he had to find some relief; so between innings he slipped into the clubhouse to calm his nerves with a quick beer. It did the job; but a couple innings later, he got jumpy again, and once again ducked inside for a beer.

Unfortunately, this was observed by one of the coaches for the opposing team, and it gave him an idea. A couple innings later, with the game tied and Famey about to go to the mound again, the coach figured Mel would be going in for one more gulp of fortitude. He slipped into the clubhouse himself, and doctored Mel's beer with a mild tranquilizer. It wasn't very powerful— just enough to take the speed off Mel's famous fastball, and loosen up his control. It did the job: Famey walked three men in a row, and then proceeded to walk in the winning run.

As he cowered in the locker room in dejection, the winning team came barging in, ready to celebrate. One of the opposing players made a grab for the beer; but the coach, who was in the know, had to stop him: "Don't touch that," he said. "That's the beer that made Mel Famey walk us."

Thanks to Scot Whitney

MEDITERRANEAN ROMANCE

Before becoming a poet, the famous Omar Khayyam was a well-to-do merchant, it's said. He amassed a fortune greater than that of the caliph—and therein lay a problem, for the caliph was easily jealous. Omar hoped to protect his wealth from the caliph's itching palm by buying into the ruby market. He purchased thousands of the precious stones; but the caliph caught on to him, and hatched a new plot to seize Omar's holdings for the national treasury. Omar decided to get the rubies out of the country fast, so he purchased a large sailing vessel and loaded the gems aboard. He hired a crew and the ship set sail; and that was the maiden voyage of the legendary Ruby Yacht of Omar Khayyam.

THE PRODIGAL SON

A father was growing weary of his son's profligate ways. The boy, an inveterate gambler, kept running up debts; and though he worked in the old man's firm and was able from time to time to get ahead of his debts by allowing his father to garnish his salary, it was a continually frustrating cycle for the old man. He finally went to his attorney. "I want to disown the boy," he announced. "That's the only way I can keep from being responsible for the horrendous damage I know he's going to do me one of these days." The attorney balked. "But what about the debts he's already got? Why not keep him on a little longer, so he won't be leaving you owing." "I thought of that," said the father. "But I can't handle the kid any more. In the end, I decided it's easier debt than son."

A LONG WALK

"Step on a crack and you break your mother's back," goes the old rhyme; and though there's probably nothing to it, it guides the way many of us walk down the street for years after we outgrow childish games. I knew one fellow who became obsessed with not only avoiding cracks but counting them. One day on the waterfront, he tried a new variation. Instead of counting cracks along the concrete, he decided to pace off the slits between the boards of the pier. He headed down the pier, counting the slits—and, of course, to do this, he had to keep looking down, intently. This precluded his seeing where he was going, and, as you've probably guessed, he fell off the end of the pier. What you *haven't* guessed, I'll bet, is what he said when he came to the surface: "Aha!" he announced triumphantly, wagging a finger in the air; "When you're out of slits, you're out of pier!"

A bandleader was bent on developing his orchestra into a novelty act—the most unusual band in the country. He was well on his way, with all kinds of odd instruments, strange vocal talents, and the like. But he was beside himself when he heard of a farmer with a herd of musical cows. Every cow played a different instrument, and he'd actually trained them to play several tunes, on key and in harmony. The bandleader had to hear them for himself; and when he did, he was amazed. "Magnificent!" he cried. "I must have them! I'll meet any price."

"I'm afraid it's not as simple as that," said the farmer's agent. "Sure, he'll hire his cows out to you, all right. But you've got to deal with him in the right mood." The bandleader was curious: "What do you mean?" The agent explained, "Well, he's pretty eccentric. Before you do business with him, he's going to want you to take a little marijuana with him." The bandleader sighed with relief. "Is that all? Easiest thing in the world!" "Don't be so sure," said the agent. "He uses it in a funny way. Suppositories."

The bandleader was stunned. "I never even *heard* of marijuana suppositories!"

The agent was apologetic. "I hate to have to be this way," he said, "but the farmer does business only on his own terms, however odd they may be." After a time, the bandleader decided to go along with it. "After all," he figured, "a herd in the band is worth boo in the tush."

AFTER THE DELUGE

Two supply clerks were caught in the office supply company's warehouse when the water main burst and began flooding the entire building. Their access to the exit was cut off; and though they phoned for help, and new rescue was at hand, they were at a loss as to how to keep themselves warm and dry until the rescue team arrived. One fellow wrapped himself in roll after roll of blotting paper; but as the water rose, it continued to soak through the makeshift blanket, and the guy got drenched through and through. The other clerk had found a large wooden crate and had dumped out its contents and climbed in. At the end of the ordeal, he emerged warm, dry and comfortable. He'd even managed to sleep through some of the flood. It all goes to show, once again, that wood is thicker than blotter.

Professor Stein, testing his time machine, was astounded to discover just what H.G. Wells had prognosticated: A race of future creatures, horrible and grasping, who attempted to chase him back into the present, and so overtake *our* world as well as their own. Making good his escape from this horrible future, he sprang into his time machine, but not before several of the horrible creatures had attached themselves to it. Contact, evidently, was sufficient to cause the creatures to be swept along, through time, with Professor Stein and his machine. With their sharp, file-like claws, the monsters began to scrape away at the machine, and Stein had real fears that they'd get inside, devour him, and appropriate the machine for their own uses. The thought made him shudder; and then he tried an alternative course of action. He reset the gauge on his machine, which had been set for a return to the 1980s, and brought his machine to a momentary halt— not in any time at all, but *outside* of time! "A sort of time travelers' rest area," Stein explained later; "an odd sort of pocket outside the main flow of temporal continuity— there are such things, and thank God for it! Because I was inside my machine, I was cushioned against the kind of pressure exerted in such an out-of-time zone, and so survived quite comfortably. But the creatures, because they were outside time itself, were nowhere (perhaps I should say no-*when*), and so they simply ceased to exist. Once they'd gone, I returned safely to the present."

The headline on the newspaper's account of the event: A NICHE IN TIME SAVES STEIN.

TWO INJURIES

It was a big job, stripping the old paint off an entire house and sanding it clean. Hard to imagine two guys taking it on, but that's how they tackled it: One man stripping, the other sanding, all under the supervision of a foreman, who was also keeping track of several other jobs.

Unfortunately, the man doing the stripping was also something of a tippler. He was fine until lunch; but he drank his noonday repast, and was seriously intoxicated before the end of the lunch break. In fact, he was so drunk that when a bit of his Bloody Mary spilled on his wrist he thought it was real blood, and went running to the First Aid man.

Now the First Aid man was one of the other workers, and he had a job to do. He wasn't about to be bothered by this drunk with his phony injury. So he simply took out a piece of facial tissue and gave it to the drunk. "Here's some gauze," he said. "Slap that on it, and go home for the rest of the day." It was all right to send him home, because he was too drunk to be of any use on the job anyway; so the fellow staggered away smiling, holding the tissue on his tomato-stained wrist.

As luck would have it, though, the fellow doing the sanding, who was quite sober, sustained a *real* injury. He got his fingers caught in the belt of his sanding machine and cut them deeply. He ran bleeding to the First Aid man, who impatiently pulled out another facial tissue and said, "Here's some gauze!" The foreman was aghast when he saw this, and he immediately confronted the First Aid man.

"It was all right to do that with the drunk," he said, "because he wasn't really hurt, and too drunk to know the difference anyway. But this man is really injured!"

"So what?" asked the First Aid man. "What's gauze for the souse is gauze for the sander."

STAGE DIRECTIONS

An unusually large woman purchased a ticket for a stagecoach out of St. Louis; but when it came time to board, the agent stopped her. "I'm sorry, ma'am, but you can't get on," he said. "Why not?" she asked. "Well, y'see, ma'am, it's your . . . your posterior." "What?!" asked the woman, shocked. "You see," the agent explained with embarrassment, "we've got strict rules. We can't let anybody on the stage if his behind is too wide. It cuts down on the number of passengers we can accomodate, and interferes with the comfort of others."

When the woman recovered from her indignation, she offered to purchase two tickets, but the agent refused. "I'm sorry, ma'am, but rules are rules." "But," she blustered, "how am I going to get to Dodge City?" "I guess you're not, ma'am," said the agent. "I s'pose there's no West for the reary."

HAUTE COUTURE

A world-famous designer scored the coup of his life when he created a brand new fabric. "This is the greatest thing since Qiana!" said one of his helpers; to which he scornfully replied, "Nothing so tacky as Qiana, darling! This is the elegant end—a quality fabric that everyone who's anyone will be wearing next season!"

The designer set his sights on introducing the new fabric at a grand ball, where a dress of the stuff would be worn by none other than Brooke Shields. Unfortunately, a couple days before the ball, a delivery man got the information wrong and delivered the dress to Brooke Adams! When Brooke Shields called up asking where her dress was, the designer was most apologetic, and ordered his staff to work overtime to prepare a replacement for the missing dress and get it to her on time. The designer still didn't know what had become of the first dress, but he was letting nothing stand in the way of the introduction of his new fabric!

Alas! On the night of the ball, both Miss Shields *and* Miss Adams showed up wearing identical dresses. So mortifying was the experience—for them *and* the other folks at the party—that the designer's hour of triumph was turned to shame, and his new fabric, as well as his career, went down the drain. Which all goes to demonstrate the veracity of the old adage: Too many Brookes spoil the cloth.

EXISTENTIALISM REVISITED

"Reading Jean Paul Sartre's *Nausea* got me so depressed and world-weary!" one college student said to another. "I felt the physical pain of that book—so much so that I didn't know what I should read next, to sort of get me out of that mood."

"What did you finally decide on?" the other asked.

"*Being and Nothingness.*"

"What? You were upset by *Nausea*, so you turned right around and read another book by Sartre?"

"Yes—it was sort of a case of indulging in Sartre for Sartre's ache."

Inspector Mugwump was at it again. In no time at all, he'd captured the notorious and feared criminal who had been molesting women viciously for some weeks in the West End. Turned out he was an escaped sexual psychopath named Simon Grath, and he was quickly returned to the hospital, where he was placed under maximum security confinement. "That wraps up that case," Mugwump told Sergeant Bowser; "and I have the perfect name for the file, too."

"What would that be, sir?" asked Bowser.

"I thought you'd have guessed, Bowser," replied Mugwump. "We'll call it 'The Rapes of Grath.'"

He didn't have much of a rest, though. The Yard immediately put him on the case of the mysterious disappearance of the British Museum's entire collection of jade pieces. Inspector Mugwump seemed instinctively to know just where to go. He directed Sergeant Bowser to drive him to the Nunn Public School, where he demanded to see the Headmaster. As they awaited the arrival of that august personage, Bowser scratched his head. "How do you know this has anything to do with the missing jade, sir?"

"This Headmaster may not actually *have* the jade, Bowser," said Mugwump, "but I'm sure it all passed through here. We're on the trail of it, there's no doubt about that."

"Why do you say so, sir?"

"Simple, Bowser: The track of all jades is the Master of Nunn."

A HUMBLE SERVANT

A humble servant of the Lord was Old Barnabas, who had been the custodian at Saint Swithin's Church for many years. Now he was pretty much retired, having long since passed the age for mopping, painting, window washing, and the like. But he still lived on the premises and supervised the younger custodians in their work, keeping to himself two main jobs: Locking and unlocking the doors, and taking care of the church's seating arrangements. You might say that all Barnabas had to do was mind his keys and pews.

SCREEN TEST

It was an exotic spectacle they were shooting, and in the key scene the star would have to leap through a secret passage in the knee of a huge sacred statue, into the realm of an evil ruler named Kevin. This would precipitate a dramatic and action-packed battle between the hero and the villain that would bring about the climax of the film.

Two stars were testing for the part of the hero: Mark Hamill and Mitchell Ryan. Ultimately the role had to be awarded on a purely physical basis. Ryan just had too much trouble performing the trick involving the statue; and because of the way the shot was set up, they couldn't use a stunt man. Because Hamill could do the stunt himself, he got the part. The producer justified the decision this way: "It is easier for Hamill to pass through the knee of an idol than for Mitch Ryan to enter the kingdom of Kevin."

ELEMENTARY

After the case of *The Hound of the Baskervilles* had been solved, Dr. Watson asked Holmes how he had found the location of the Great Grimpen Mire so easily. "Elementary, my dear Watson," replied the sleuth. "I just looked for a crowd of people and there it was!"

"A crowd of people? I don't understand."

"My good man, haven't you heard the saying? Where there's folk, there's mire."

SCHOOLBOY IN LOVE

A college lad became hopelessly enamored of a young lady in one of his classes. So moonstruck was he that his work in that course began to suffer. He spent all his time gazing at his beloved, and was consequently inattentive in class. He knew that if he was going to pass the course at all he'd have to transfer to a different section, thereby eliminating his distraction and improving his performance. However, to do so would mean to deprive himself of the daily vision of loveliness that he'd come to look forward to. In the end, he decided to stay in the same class so he could see her every day, regardless of the impact it might have on his work. It was a clear case of putting the heart before the course.

THE DRUNKEN BARBARIAN

Odd, isn't it, how many of our stories involve drink and drinking? It may be because so many of our euphemisms and slang words pertain to that much enjoyed but much maligned and long "forbidden" pleasure. This quickie tells us of the right-hand man of the young Attila. Attila was little more than a teenager at the time, and had not yet risen to power, though everyone who knew him was sure that great things were in store for him. His close friend was sure, too, and thought that by attaching himself to Attila, he would ensure for himself a place of influence and power when his friend became king. Unfortunately, he took too much to the soft life, drinking heavily, and the shrewd Attila was never willing to trust him in a position of any importance. Nevertheless, the drunk was a merry companion, and Attila kept him around for laughs. He was known derisively around the tribe as "The Souse of the Rising Hun."

73

CLEANING HOUSE

Weeding out unneeded possessions was an annual spring ritual at the H's house, and this year Mrs. H, especially had a lot to get rid of. In particular, she had cottoned to the new fashion of carrying a small, dainty purse, and now saw fit to dispose of the several large purses she had kept in years past. These she discarded into a large pile, to be taken to the rummage sale. Her husband and a neighbor stood looking at the heap for a moment. Then the neighbor reflected, "There's a great lesson here." The husband was puzzled. "What do you mean?" he asked. The neighbor was surprised. "Why surely," he said, "you've heard of the Parable of the Pile of Great Purse!"

STILL IN THE BUSINESS

A legendary brothel owner, so pre-eminent
in the trade that everyone knew her simply as "Madam," used to operate a high-
class establishment in Peking. With the
coming of the Chinese Revolution, she had
to go into hiding; but in a year or so she
resurfaced in Shanghai, where she opened
a smaller place. It was an unassuming
business, operating out of a dingy little
hut; but Madam had the touch of gold,
and the best clients still sought her out.
To this day, her praises are sung by a
loyal group of admirers who speak know-
ingly of "Madam's Shanghai Shack."

CANADIAN HONKER

A Mountie in the far North had little company, so his best friends became his sled dogs and a playful Canadian goose that came along for the ride. He didn't know about the goose at first, and the way he found out was curious. As he mushed his way through the snows, he kept hearing this "honk-honk!" He was hundreds of miles from any real traffic, and thought maybe snow-fever had made him begin to hallucinate. "Honk-honk!" came the noise again and again. He finally found the goose, but not before crying out in anguish, "Who's been beeping in my sled?"

CATHEDRALE ENGLOUTIE

There is absolutely no truth to the rumor that Claude Debussy's haunting piano piece "The Sunken Cathedral" was originally a dance tune titled "Ringin' in the Seine."

CICERONEAN MENU

The proprietor of a Japanese restaurant developed a unique house specialty, a combination of batter-fried shrimp and vegetables and marinated eels. The dish became quite popular and was always in demand. One day, when he'd run out of a couple of key ingredients, and couldn't offer the dish, the proprietor put up a sign that read: "Sorry. No Tempura, No Morays."

EDAM NEAR GOT KILLED

Two friends were hitchhiking and were picked up by the driver of a huge grocery truck. There was little room in front, but he was willing to let them ride in back with the cargo, and they were happy to get the ride. Their happiness was short-lived, however, for the driver turned out to be a real cowboy: The truck swerved, bounced, and sped along the highway to the point where the hitchhikers were begging for a chance to get out. They couldn't, however; and a few miles further on they knew the driver had finally done it: They felt the truck swerve off the road and tip over. The crashes were deafening as the truck rolled over and over and over, finally coming to rest. In the dark cargo area of the truck, one hitchhiker whispered to the other, "You all right?" "Yes," came the reply. They discovered that they had been cushioned by some soft cargo, and had escaped injury. Moments later, the cargo door was opened; light poured in; and the hitchhikers saw the source of their salvation: Several boxes of assorted cheese had cushioned the impact of the accident and allowed them to escape injury. "Whew!" said one to the other: "What a friend we have in cheeses."

A NEW TV SHOW

One of the glories of the coming television season, rumor has it, will be a cop show with a difference. This one is about a police dog—an Alaskan Malamute who stops crooks by squirting them with Vano. The title? "Husky and Starch."

HABERDASHERY

A department store owner was dissatisfied with the inefficiency of the clothing departments in his store. "It's because of the counter," one of the clerks told him. "It doesn't allow us enough space to work. We have to pile the clothes up on the counter, and it slows us down." So the owner ordered a new style of counter for the clothing department. This kind had a vertical post with a hanger arrangement attached. "There," he told the head clothing clerk. "Now you won't have to pile clothes on the counter; you can hang them up." After a few days, though, efficiency was worse than ever. "The clothes hang in our faces when we're trying to work," complained the clerk. "It's even worse than it was before." Undaunted, the department store owner went to a fixture designer and got yet another model of counter, in which there was plenty of space to work and the hanger-apparatus was well out of the way of the work area. Within days, efficiency increased several hundred percent. Delighted, the owner notified all his clothing departments that they should immediately order and install clothing counters of the third kind.

A SPANISH TRAGEDY

There was a terrible mine disaster in the Basque Region of Spain. No one was injured in the actual cave-in; and the hundreds of Basque miners who were in the mine when the collapse occurred weren't even trapped. They had two avenues of escape from the mine. Unfortunately, in their panic, they all crowded into the closest passage, and in the crush several dozen needless deaths resulted. The moral of the story? Don't put all your Basques in one exit.

REJOINDER

A stuffy professor was regaling one of his fellows with tales of his own achievements. "The secret of my positive outlook on life is just this," he said. "Each morning I get up and start the day by reading a few lines from Wordsworth." "Good God," replied the listener, "that's going from bed to verse!"

MORE FROM MUGWUMP

Inspector Mugwump set right to work on the case of Lady Dogwell's missing emerald necklace. "Sergeant Bowser," he ordered his assistant, "I want you to bring in for questioning every known felon and every nursemaid in the city—but only those under five-feet four."

"But, sir," protested Bowser, "this is a case of a missing item of jewelry. How will this plan help you to solve it?"

"Simple," said Mugwump. "I'm going to find this missing necklace if I have to examine every little crook and nanny."

A few days later, when the questioning had proved fruitless, Inspector Mugwump went back to Lady Dogwell, and learned something new. "I *did* take a boat trip last week," she told him, "and I suppose it's *possible* that the necklace fell off into the water . . ."

"Aha!" exclaimed Mugwump. "You should have told me earlier, m'lady!" With that he set off on a new tack, enigmatically ordering Sergeant Bowser to obtain immediately x-rays of all fish landed for marketing in the past week.

"This is just what I was looking for!" Mugwump announced the next day, when he saw the x-ray of a large shark with a dark spot in its stomach. He ordered that the shark be seized and cut open; and sure enough, there lay Lady Dogwell's necklace!

The Lady was overjoyed—but puzzled. "How did you do it?"

"Just luck, really," Mugwump said modestly. "It was a dot in the shark."

BABY, IT'S COLD OUTSIDE

Joe, Ed, and Bill were the members of a research team sent into the bitterest part of the Arctic one winter to gather meteorological data. Alas, someone had miscalculated, and their provisions began to run short before the project was half over. To make matters worse, when they tried to radio home-base for more supplies, they found their communications system had gone dead. Under these suddenly strenuous conditions, they had to take extreme measures. They began to ration their food carefully, assuming that after a few days of no communication, home-base would wonder about them and send someone to check on them. But as the days went by, and the hunger mounted, no help was forthcoming. Finally, Bill could take it no longer. He desperately ran out into the deadly frozen night in a crazed effort to escape. Joe and Ed found him the next day not 400 yards from camp, frozen solid. They carried him back to camp, but agreed that the best thing to do was to keep him frozen, the better to preserve his body for the sad trip home, when rescue came. So Bill's stiffened body was kept standing just outside the door to their hut against the day they would all be heading back. Still no help came; and even with only two of them to share the food, provisions grew treacherously low. At last Joe and Ed agreed they'd have to do the unthinkable: Use Bill's frozen body for food, to get them through a few more days. Neither, however, had the heart to be the first to violate the dignity of the corpse; so finally they agreed to take a bite out of their dead comrade simultaneously. Joe munched into one side as Ed gnawed the other. Ed was obviously upset and sickened by the deed; Joe, on the other hand, was a tough, practical sort of guy, who kept his sense of humor in all situations. It didn't fail him now; and he tried to cheer Ed up with the remark, "I'd call that a Billsicle bite for two."

ARCHAEOLOGICAL FIND

Two archaeologists were sifting through the dirt of an ancient ruin. One told the other, "I need to find the missing piece—or pieces—to an exquisite urn I've been reconstructing. I've found and reassembled nearly all the pieces, but there's still a hole. I'm guessing by the design that the missing piece shows the face of a leopard. At least his body is on the urn, just below the hole." The two worked in silence for a long time. Then the other archaeologist gasped, concentrated a moment, worked feverishly with his broom, and finally came up with a large fragment of pottery. He gave it to the other man, who examined it, then smiled broadly. Do you know what he said next? You ought to: "The shard is my leopard!"

BIG · P·VSSYCAT ·

STRATEGY CONFERENCE

Several Allied generals were discussing their plans for the upcoming invasion; but the conference got sidetracked when a dispute arose. "My men are to mass in grid square B-2," said one general, only to be quickly interrupted by another general. "No, no—it's B-3," the latter said. As it happened, the one who interrupted was a longtime rival of the general who was speaking, and the two had little patience with each other. The first general shot back, "Who are you to interrupt me?" "Only one who feels he has to correct incompetence at any level," replied the second general. "Incompetence!" blustered the first, "Why, you upstart!" Recrimination followed recrimination; until at last the Chief of Staff had to break up the argument. "Gentlemen," he shouted, "don't let this get down to personalities. Stick to the point!: B-2 or *not* B-2—*that* is the question!"

REIGN OF TERROR

The nobility knew the revolution would suc
ceed; but they couldn't believe that their way
of life was gone forever. After all, hadn't the
monarchy been restored in England after
only a few short years of Cromwell? So they
banded together and agreed on a hiding
place for the largest portion of their accumulated wealth, where it could be saved for
the "restoration" that they, too, hoped for.

Two rival factions controlled the revolu-
tionary government, and they fought each
other bitterly; but they agreed on one thing:
Their hatred for the nobility. Both factions set about rounding up the lords and
nobles of the realm. Pierre, the leader
of the more extreme faction, summarily
marched the nobles off to the axe. But the
leader of the other faction, Jacques, was
of a less hardheaded temperament. He
brought a few of the nobles before him and
told them of the horrible tortures he had in
store for them. It was only a matter of time
before one of them broke down and agreed
to tell Jacques the hiding place of the
wealth, in exchange for sparing his life.
That was how Jacques managed to acquire
fortune and power, and how his faction even-
tually wiped Pierre's faction off the map.

The moral of the story: Don't hatchet
your counts before they chicken.

Thanks to Scot Whitney

COVEN

George was not appalled when he found out his friend Frank Lee was a prominent member of a witches' coven. On the contrary, he was fascinated, and wondered if he could see some of the activities of the group. Frank was happy to oblige, up to a point, but stopped short of allowing George access to the coven's highest secrets. George's appetite and curiosity were whetted, however, and he decided to work his way up to becoming one of the initiate. "You must be prepared to do whatever is asked of you," Frank told him, as the time of George's confirmation drew nearer. At last, George was allowed into the inner circle. What a letdown! He was critically disappointed when he discovered the high priest to be nothing more than a pathetic little man wearing a deer's head. And then, for the first time, George was genuinely appalled when he learned what was expected of him. "Brother George," intoned the high priest, "to become one of our number you must perform a scarifice to me, the sylvan god. The sacrifice must be your own mother." A more profligate soul might have been tempted to go through with the grisly deed, but George drew the line. He told his friend in no uncertain terms, "Frank Lee, I don't give a deer my dam."

CRITICS' NIGHT OUT

Three movie reviewers were going out to a premiere one night in the '60s, and had agreed to share a ride. The first picked up the second, then drove to the home of the third, who was none other than Bosley Crowther, of the New York Times. They arrived outside Crowther's apartment building; but, though they were late, Bosley was not waiting for them out front as he had promised. "Perhaps he's still upstairs," suggested the rider to the driver. "Why not give a toot on the horn?" The driver was indignant. "Certainly not," he replied. "Am I my Crowther's beeper?"

WHEN KNIGHTHOOD WAS IN FLOWER

It's not well known, but there were female knights. Not many, of course; but a few of these feminists-before-their-time once rode the British isles on chivalric missions, back in the distant past when dragons still prowled and magic was alive in the land. One such was the noble Sir Pamela, who set out to become the most famous knight in the realm by taking on the deadly Sussex Serpent. This ferocious dragon was particularly feared because it was rumored to have seven lives. A valiant dragonslayer might easily meet his (or her) death by dispatching the dragon only to be gobbled up when the dragon came suddenly back to life. This had already happened, in fact— but Sir Pamela didn't know how often it had happened, and so had no idea how many of the dragon's lives were used up. So, armed to the teeth and keeping herself continually vigilant, she went up against the dragon. Each time the monster collapsed in death, she kept her guard up, ready to do combat anew when the beast rose up. Try as it might, the dragon couldn't fool her, and she killed it again and again until it died for the final time. Upon re-

ceiving congratulations and thanks from the appreciative king, Sir Pamela shyly acknowledged that she could never have done it without the crowd of supporters that stood on the sidelines, cheering her on. Each time she killed the dragon, they shouted their encouragement. The cry that bore her up? You guessed it: "Slay it again, Pam!"

AT THE CABARET

Fred and Larry went out for a night at the cabaret, where a middle eastern dancer was performing, and they were most appreciative of the show. So enthused was Larry, in fact, that he wanted to tip the dancer a cool ten dollars. Now there's a right way to tip a belly dancer: You fold the bill, and hold it up; when she dances near you, you slip it into the beltline of her skirt. Larry, alas, didn't know this, and kept waving his money clumsily around, to the distaste of the dancer, and to the embarrassment of Fred, who finally decided to enlighten him. Said he: "That's the wrong way to tip'er, Larry."

THE MIRACLE

You may already be aware of what the disciples said, on the occasion of the Miracle of the Loaves and the Fishes: "Oh, Lord! What foods these morsels be!"

THE HELL'S ANGLES' TRADE FAIR

Part of the annual convention and encampment of the Hell's Angels was a flea market and trading fair. Big Luke came with the hope of picking himself up a new bike through shrewd trading. After several tries, he finally found an Angel he figured he could get the best of. Sure enough, Little Pete was no good at all at the fine art of haggling, and Big Luke got the better of the deal. "Where'd you score the new hog?" his friends wanted to know, and Big Luke was quick to inform them, proudly, "I got it off Little Pete. His barter's worse than his bike."

CRAZY MAN

He was just a freelance accountant. He charged a modest fee, but the clients didn't come. He found it impossible to make a living from his meager earnings, and the stress drove him stark-raving mad. His closest friend—the only one, it seemed, who was concerned about him—finally caught up with him at a nearby funny farm, where he had centered his attentions on a new hobby that seemed to calm his disordered mind: riding a calf and splashing paint on anything that might come near. His friend tried to find the sense in this. He recognized that there was little point in trying to find sense in the actions of a madman; but he had to admit there was method in the accountant's madness, when the crazy man replied, "It's better to dye on your neat than live on your fees."

SONS OF TOIL

The farmers of a certain district were concerned about the declining productivity of their soil. The last couple seasons just hadn't been what they should, and so these earnest agrarians summoned the assistance of the Department of Agriculture. The expert who came to inspect the land told them their problem was lack of aeration. "Your soil's losing oxygen," he said, "and it's becoming too dense to grow crops in. You have to find a way of aerating it, providing new pockets of air to allow growing room and provide subterranean oxygen."

The expert puzzled on the problem for a few days, and then announced he had a solution. "I'll probe the earth here and there," he said, "until I find an air pocket—there are always lots of pockets of air under pressure inside the earth. When I find one, I'll simply penetrate it by sinking a shaft and applying a pump apparatus. This will enable us to harness the air under pressure and use it to aerate all the surrounding land, just like a well is used to provide water."

The structure he proposed was soon built, the soil was aerated, the land began to produce as before, and the Agriculture man went on his way. "What was that guy's name, anyway?" one of the farmers asked another. "I don't know," the other replied, "but it must've been Hemingway." "Hemingway?" asked the first. "What makes you say that?" "Well, because he created an airwell to farms!"

THE HIGHER TECHNOLOGY

What did the mathematical computer say to its operator? "Sum up and key me sometime."

ES WAR EINMAL

A heat wave in Saxony caused a pig farmer to become concerned about the sudden sluggishness of his stock. The veterinarian came as quickly as he could and examined the pigs. Their lack of sweat, he knew, was a sign of severe heatstroke, and he set about to cool and moisten them at the well. Alas, he found that the pump was jammed, and he could draw only a dribble of water. He went hurriedly to the farmer and explained the situation: "Swine dry, I fear. Pump sticks. Seepin'." To which the farmer replied, in despair, "Ach! Annoying scene!"

ENGLAND SWING LIKE A PENDULUM DO

Back in the days of the Swinging London of the '60s, when the entire city was divided between the Mods and the Rockers, a certain wealthy man was eager to impress his son, a Mod, with how hip he was. Trouble was, he didn't quite understand what it was that the nattily-dressed rebel stood for. Not social consciousness, certainly: For when the man invited a poor, homeless street urchin in to dine with him and his son, the young man stomped out in anger. "Why?" the old man wanted to know. "Don't you know?" asked the boy. "You cannot serve both Mod and gamin!"

THE WRECK OF
THE *HELEN*

The *Helen*, a proud cargo ship, was coming into port with her freight: A load of expensive and beautiful vases from the Greek Isles, to be offered at great price in American galleries—the kind of thing that would delight collectors and connoisseurs. The import magnate who was overseeing the operation was so pleased that he decided to impart an atmosphere of pomp and ceremony to the docking of the *Helen*. To this end, he dispatched a motor launch with several welcoming dignitaries aboard to greet the ship. His plan backfired, however: The skipper of the launch was preoccupied talking with one of the passengers, and steered his little vessel right into the path of the *Helen*. The freighter veered aside, missing the launch by inches, but causing her cargo to become unstable. In the hold, boxes and crates crashed all around; and when the final analysis was complete more than a thousand of the precious pottery works lay damaged. The launch skipper was immediately fired and sent away; but this did not appease the magnate, who also ordered the launch permanently retired. She was put into

drydock, and for years afterward, passersby would look at her in wonder and ask, "Was this the launch that chipped a thousand vases?"

A PRELUDE TO THE FINALE

What was it they said when the giants for
Helsinki entered the room? :
  "Here come the big Finnish folks!"

A HOLIDAY REVEL

A prosperous pea-farmer decided to throw a big Christmas party along the ridge where he has his property. The guest list was one of the most diverse ever known.

Executives of the six largest corporations in the country each brought their wives, but it was clear that they had a condescending attitude about the whole thing. They were coming only to watch the quaint lower classes deporting themselves in amusing ways. As a result, the top-drawer set had a bad time of it. To make matters worse, they brought some punch laced with a bad hallucinogen, and they all had bad trips.

Dyspeptic gossip columnists from eleven papers were invited, and were so worked up by the goings-on that they began writing their columns right there, each trying to scoop the other with the latest dirt.

The main actor and actress of each of five new films were all invited, and by an outrageous coincidence all of them ran off to get married at the height of the festivities.

Nine of the world's ten best-dressed men showed up, and all wore the very latest shoe design. Unfortunately, it wasn't perfected yet: The shoes kept coming untied and they spent a lot of their time retying them.

Booked in for entertainment was a double quartet of mid-range sopranos. Not wishing to strain their voices, they sang in a low tone of voice, and could scarcely be heard.

A local spiritualist cult sent seven representatives, but these quasi-gurus had too much to drink and quickly turned to chasing women all night.

Half a dozen carnival freaks were hanging around the punchbowl when one of the guests took off her cape and whirled it around like a matador, challenging one of the men to charge her; whereupon the carnival guys filled out the tableau by cheering like a bullfight crowd.

It was December, and the host felt reasonably sure that the ice would stay frozen even outside; but it was sultry for that time of year, and the ice melted, so only the first five guests actually got cold drinks. All the rest were lukewarm.

Two oversexed couples from Kurdistan dropped by, but spent their whole time making love in the bushes.

A troupe of midget acrobats, particularly close pals of the farmer though they were only a quarter of a foot tall, came by to spend some time. The farmer looked after his little buddies to make sure they didn't get stepped on.

At the peak of the excitement, one of the ladies dropped her gloves in the dirt, and before she could retrieve them they were trampled by reveling guests. This upset her so much that she made a big issue of it, and it became one of the high points of the party, as recounted by a poetically inclined columnist:

Twelve slummers bumming, eleven snipers typing, ten leads eloping, nine dandies lacing, eight mezzos marking, seven swamis sinning, six geeks olé-ing, five cold drinks, four balling Kurds, three-inch friends, two dirty gloves at the party on the pea-ridge.